Francis Frith

Lower Egypt, Thebes and the pyramids

Francis Frith

Lower Egypt, Thebes and the pyramids

ISBN/EAN: 9783742844965

Manufactured in Europe, USA, Canada, Australia, Japa

Cover: Foto ©ninafisch / pixelio.de

Manufactured and distributed by brebook publishing software (www.brebook.com)

Francis Frith

Lower Egypt, Thebes and the pyramids

LOWER EGYPT, THEBES,

AND

THE PYRAMIDS.

BY

FRANCIS FRITH.

LONDON:
WILLIAM MACKENZIE, 22 PATERNOSTER ROW;
GLASGOW, AND EDINBURGH.

OSIRIDÆ PILLARS AND FALLEN COLOSSUS,

AT THE MEMNONIUM, THEBES.

WHAT a marvellously quaint period in the world's history was the time of Rameses the Great (about 1300 years before Christ), with its unlettered wisdom, its self-originated arts, its vigorous but rude civilization! Unacquainted with a remote Past, it laboured to build up for itself an immortal Future. I wonder how many representations of him — statues and sculptures — the great Rameses executed in the course of his long and brilliant reign of fifty-five years; certainly some hundreds still exist in Egypt, and I suppose there is hardly a capital in Europe which does not boast at least one of his portraits. His features are calm and majestic, if not handsome, with no approach to the negro character, especially in the lips. The great figures of the façade at Abou Simbel are his finest representatives, the faces being almost angelic in their calm and happy dignity of expression.

But the largest, and probably the most beautiful colossal statue ever produced, was erected by this monarch at the Memnonium (more correctly called the Rameseum), at Thebes. My Photograph gives the principal fragment of this statue as it now lies, and as it has in all probability lain since the time of the Persian conquest. This fragment (the size of which should be compared with the living figures grouped around it) is merely the head and shoulders of the figure, which was of one single block of syenite granite, and is computed to have weighed about 900 tons. It represented the king seated upon a throne, in an attitude of repose, and was probably intended to commemorate his victorious return from the warlike campaigns with which an Egyptian monarch usually commenced his reign. David Roberts, in his splendid work, has bestowed upon it a very respectable and recognisable profile; but my picture shows that the face is so mutilated as scarcely to leave a feature traceable. Its proportions, however, are the marvel. It weighed, when perfect, three times as much as the largest obelisk in Egypt, and was brought from a distance of about 100 miles. History presents but one grander project for the gratification of a monarch's vanity, viz., that of the architect Dinocrates, who proposed to Alexander to cut Mount Athos into a statue of the king, holding in one hand a city of 10,000 inhabitants, and from the other pouring a copious river into the sea. But if we are astonished by the first successes of the Egyptian king, we are scarcely less perplexed as to the means employed for its destruction. I am reminded of an inscription which is found upon some of the Nile temples, to the effect that only he who succeeds in destroying it, will be a mightier man than the founder. The lower parts of the Rameseum statue are entirely destroyed, and reduced to mere fragments; the upper part (which is shown in my picture), broken off at the waist, is merely thrown back upon the ground, and probably remains as it first fell. There are no marks of wedges in the fragments; gunpowder seems to be the only means with which we are acquainted that could produce similar results. Sir G. Wilkinson says, "The figures seen across the head and on the pedestal are the work of a later period, when some of the pieces were cut for millstones by the Arabs."

THE RAMESEUM, THEBES.

The traveller who is "doing" Thebes quickly, usually "makes" first for those great land-marks—Statues of Memnon. Leaving them, he bears a little to the right, having in view, at a distance of about a mile, the Temple of the Rameseum, or, as it is more commonly called, the Memnonium. He winds round the dilapidated pylon, and soon encounters the great fallen Colossus, which is the chief subject of our previous picture. Then he enters the Hall of Columns (to be described by and bye), and passing through it he emerges on the right hand, or north side, upon a space strewn with broken masonry, and which at a little distance from the Temple, is occupied by a series of crude brick vaults of considerable antiquity, and which have probably been used as dwellings. From the top of these vaults is obtained the fine view of the Temple, now presented to the reader. The sun is sinking towards the west, and will soon be below the mountains which rise boldly at our back, and which are completely honey-combed with tombs—thousands of them have been laid open and ransacked by the Arabs.

The Rameseum is one of the most important ruins of Thebes. Speaking of it, Sir Gardner Wilkinson (than whom, in spite of all that has been since written, we have perhaps no more correct and reliable authority) says—"For symmetry of architecture and elegance of sculpture, there is no doubt that this temple may vie with any other monument of Egyptian art." Yet it is dreadfully dilapidated. You may judge by the Photographs that it is but a scrap of its former self; and it would puzzle any but an experienced eye to detect its original plan. Sir Gardner Wilkinson, in his admirable guide-book, gives the restored plan, with the remaining portions in shadow. Well-a-day! Here a column or two to represent fifty others that once surrounded the now roofless areas; there bits of the throne of a statue of black granite, whose half-dozen companions have been somehow dissipated in the general break-up; and yonder in the distance, disowning as it were any connection with the "house" over the way, is a tottering wall which was, however, some three thousand years ago, grand enough to be the enclosure of the innermost sanctuary, where the shrine of the idol stood. And here we may suitably note, that the invariable plan of an Egyptian temple "requires a diminution, but no increase of dimensions, from the entrance to the inner chambers;" so that the lofty propyla, the colonnaded areas and Halls of Columns by which the Temple-proper were approached, were always the most impressive portions of the edifice.

In the contemplation of the "Ecclesiastical" monuments of Egypt, one is filled with an exalted idea of the priest-craft of that remote day. How admirably calculated was a pylon gateway, one hundred feet high and three hundred wide, to crush into submissive littleness the ignorant and superstitious populace who passed through it! And in their progress amongst the great helgnant representations of the reigning monarch, and through hall after hall of stupendous and brilliantly-coloured columns, no wonder that by the time they reached the sanctuary they were prepared to exalt into deities the mysterious though repulsive idols to which the temple was dedicated, and to assign a scarcely inferior place to the monarch in whose honour, no less than to that of "the gods," the wonderful structure was raised.

The temple was probably known to the ancients under the name of the Tomb of Osymandyas, which is described minutely by Diodorus in terms that to a large extent suit the probable plan and condition of the Rameseum of that day. Sir Gardner Wilkinson, although admitting much of the coincidence, concludes thus—"but we may be allowed to question its having been a tomb, or having been erected by that monarch."

It only remains for me to describe the Temple. Within the now dilapidated pylon, was a court of about one hundred and eighty feet square, with two double rows of columns, and here stood the stupendous granite statue described in our previous article; another court followed, one hundred and seventy feet by one hundred and forty, surrounded by columns and Osiride pillars, and ornamented with granite statues of the founder, Rameses the Second (B.C. 1355). Hence three entrances open into the Great Hall of Columns, each with a sculptured doorway of black granite. Here were more statues of the king; twelve enormous columns, thirty-two feet high, and twenty-one feet in circumference, form a double line along the centre. There were besides eighteen smaller columns (eighteen feet in circumference) completing the total of forty-eight, and supporting its roof of enormous stones, (vide the Photograph) which was studded with stars upon an azure ground. This hall measures one hundred feet by one hundred and thirty-three. Then followed three central and six lateral chambers, of which only two now remain.—For descriptions of some of the hieroglyphic inscriptions and paintings which adorn the Rameseum, the reader is referred to the article in our Supplementary Volume which accompanies another view of this beautiful ruin.

THE TEMPLE OF GOORNEH, THEBES.

THIS Temple is, exteriorly, one of the least imposing of the ruins of Thebes. It is situated not very far from the river, amidst a grove of Tamarisk trees, and its principal feature is the portico, with a single row of pillars, represented in the view.

Goorneh was the northern district of the western half of the great city, Thebes. The remains of the Temple indicate their origin in the artistic period of Seti I. The building is styled in the hieroglyphic inscriptions there, "The magnificent Temple of Meneptkah Seti, in the City of Amun, on the west side of T'ama." Its chief apartment is a Hall, supported by six columns, from which many smaller rooms lead off. On the right and left are two larger buildings, with many chambers, which, together with their principal Hall, have all their entrances fronting the east; a colonnade extending throughout their length. The dedication on the Hall is, "Seti I. has erected this for a monument to his father, Amon Ra, the King of the Gods, and has raised for him a Temple which shall continue for millions of years, in the principal part of T'am, opposite the City of Thebes (Apé), and constructed of good white sandstone." In these and other inscriptions, the right-hand portion of the city of Thebes is often called "the Eastern T'am, or Patam," whilst the left is "the Western T'am." The city of Thebes was called Apé, with the sign of the plural at the end of this feminine proper noun.

The district on the western side of Thebes was named "the Nomos of Athor, Pa-hathor, or Pa-hathyr;" by some writers it was called "Pathyrites," or "Phaturites," and in the Bible occurs as "Pathros" (Pa-athor). It is interesting to trace, by such an "undesigned coincidence," the precise historic accuracy of the term thus used by the inspired Prophet.

Parts of the Great Hall of the Temple of Goorneh are ornamented with the representations and inscriptions of the reign of Rameses II., who completed many of the edifices which his father had commenced. In one of the paintings King Rameses II. is standing in the presence of the God Atum, and of his deceased father, Seti I. Atum addresses him thus:—"Come to me, thou, my son and offspring,—thou Horus, friend of truth,—in order that I may give thee the throne of the Sun, the Lordship of Seb, and the Kingdom of Hor." In the interior of the Temple, the God Amon appears, accompanied by his mother Mut, and her son Chonsu, together with Ptah and Athor, who is styled "Amente, Goddess of the Lower World." Amongst the names of the deities in this Temple, is the very revered one of Tuaùe, who addresses Seti I. with the words:—"I am thy mother, and I have granted thee thy beauty."

An inscription upon the left-hand door in the grand colonnade informs us that the chambers to which it leads were erected by Rameses II., who "has made this as a monument to his father, the deceased Seti I., and to his grandfather, the deceased Rameses I." In the colonnade is the date of the sixth year of Rameses II., and in other parts of it are the names of Rameses III., Meneptah Siptah, Queen Ahmes Nofertari, and King Seti I.

PYLON GATEWAY AT MEDINET-HABOO.

THE Temples of Medinet-Haboo are situated on the western bank of the Nile, and probably mark the position of the chief portion of the city of Thebes which lay on that side of the river. This group of temples and of pylon gateways, although not so impressively grand as those of Karnac, are yet of sufficient interest to class amongst the most important in Egypt.

Every age of Egyptian history is represented by one or other of these ruined piles. The place, however, is dreadfully encumbered with heaps of shapeless ruin, and still more with perfect mountains of the débris of deserted Arab towns under which the further portions of the great temple are absolutely buried. One can only guess how much more of magnificence and interest might reward the efforts of a vigorous excavating party.

We shall give, at a future time, a view of the temple-palace which first strikes the traveller as he approaches the group from the plain. Its peculiar large square windows are novelties in Egyptian architecture.

There are two principal divisions of the ruins of Medinet-Haboo, of which one is formed by the Temple of Tinthmes and the other by that of Rameses III. It is the former which is entered by that interesting Pylon Gateway which bears on its exterior the representations of the victories of the Ethiopian sovereign of Egypt, Pharaoh Taharaka, over his numerous foes, amongst whom the characteristic physiognomy of the Hebrew stamp of countenance is very conspicuous. In most places, however, the name of Taharaka has been assiduously chiselled out by some succeeding, and probably more popular and national monarch. On another part of this Pylon are the names of Nectanebus, Ptolemy Soter, and Ptolemy Philometor. The whole of the Pylon itself appears to have been built of the stones of a former Temple of Rameses II. The Temple of Tinthmes, with which this gateway was connected, bears an inscription indicating its dedication as a Hall for the religious festivals of Amen Ra. Amongst the latest records contained in it are some which bear the name of Antoninus. One of the dedicatory inscriptions on the front pylon runs thus—"The Son of the Sun, Ptolemy, the Ever-living, the Beloved of Isis, the Saviour God, has erected this for a monument to his Father, the first-created One, without whom was nothing created." Amen has a similar title in an inscription in the Temple of Apé at Karnac, but with an addition stating that he is invisible except when it is agreeable to him to manifest himself by some outward appearance. In one part of the same range at Medinet-Haboo are the colonnade and walls of a small hypæthral temple like that on the Isle of Philæ, and bearing inscriptions of the period of King Nectanebus.

But perhaps nothing will strike the traveller more, as he wanders through these wonderful ruins, than the succession of pylon gateways, leading from one immense sculptured court to another. The one now represented is, I believe, the third from the entrance. The court into which it opens has been previously depicted and described.

THE TEMPLE PALACE, MEDINET-HABOO.

To those who have followed us through our series of illustrations of ancient Egyptian architecture, the ruin here given will at once appear altogether strange and dissimilar. It is indeed unique. It was the palace of Rameses III, and is the only building of this character which has outlasted the ages of demolition and decay, to which the structures of the Nile Valley have been subjected, and nothing but proportions so prodigiously massive as to be almost immovable by human agency, has saved those that remain. This palace is, therefore, a most interesting object to the antiquarian. It is situated to the south of the Temple-Propylæ, which were erected by the same monarch, and closely contiguous to them. The square windows alone would be sufficient to distinguish it from all the other existing antiquities of Egypt. The style of its hieroglyphic embellishment is also peculiar—representing, in the interior of the chambers, various scenes of domestic life. To begin with the exterior—upon one of the wings of the building appears the king, of gigantic stature, slaughtering his enemies in battle; his divine protector, Amun Ra, extends to him the sword of victory, &c. The conquered tribes are next led into captivity, headed by their respective kings, whose countenances are very characteristic. In one of the halls is the celebrated chess-playing scene, in which the king is surrounded by his harem, one of whom he tenderly caresses, and with others he is engaged in a game which is not actually that of chess, but bears a greater resemblance to draughts. Some of his attendant ladies present him with flowers, or are engaged in fanning him; but they are all obliged to stand in his presence, the king alone being seated on an elegant divan. Sir G. Wilkinson says that the queen is not among them; and that her cartouche-oval is always blank, where it occurs, throughout the building. The game here represented is also seen in the grottoes of Beni Hassan, where it dates as far back as 1700 years before the Christian era, in the time of Osirtasin—the contemporary of Joseph. In another part of the building occur ornamented balustrades, each supported by four figures of African and northern barbarians, and the summit of the whole pavilion was crowned with a row of shields—the battlements of Egyptian architecture.

The original design of the palace was probably much more extensive than these ruins at first sight indicate. In front was a paved raised platform, and in connection with the wings were many other chambers which are now totally destroyed.

OSIRIDE PILLAR AT MEDINET-HABOO, THEBES.

THIS view represents the north-west or right-hand corner of the first great court of the Temple of Rameses III, at Medinet-Haboo. It is an hypaethral (or uncovered) area of about 140 feet by 125, having, on one side, a corridor with a row of seven Osiride pillars (one of which is included in the view), and on the other, eight circular columns with bell-shaped capitals, in imitation of the Papyrus. It is, perhaps, the most striking instance that exists, of what Sir G. Wilkinson calls the asymmetrophobia of the ancient Egyptians: the effect in this instance, at least, is not quite pleasing.

This splendid court was, on my first visit to Thebes, almost filled with rubbish, so that only the upper portions of the columns were visible. But the figure, which I photographed on my last journey, had just been uncovered by order of the Viceroy. A French artist was engaged in copying its details; and when in a few minutes, I had possessed myself of more accuracy than his labour of perhaps days would yield, he exclaimed with politeness—and (let us hope) with no dash of bitterness, nor scornfulness, nor envy —"Ah, Monsieur! que vous êtes vite, vite!"

This representation of Osiris affords a suitable opportunity to say something about the religion of ancient Egypt.

It seems to be the general opinion of the learned world, that the original and fundamental idea of the system does not embrace a polytheism; and many go so far as to assert that the worship of the Egyptians was not idolatry. In this opinion I can by no means agree. However comparatively pure may have been the belief whereupon the system with which alone we are acquainted through the hieroglyphic sculptures is based, I have no doubt that it became, at a period anterior to that of any existing monuments, as genuine and hideous an idolatry as the world ever saw. That many of the idols symbolise abstract ideas —as Power, Mercy, and the like—which may easily be supposed to be attributes of one Deity, is to sort of proof, nor scarcely argument to my mind, that they were worshipped as such. I do not doubt, for instance, that the idol which symbolized power, was regarded as the god—the supreme possessor and dispenser—of that quality; for this principle of the deification of abstract qualities or "attributes" is so obviously at the root of all idolatries, that if upon this ground we deny the Egyptian system to have been a genuine idolatry, I know not what ancient or even savage system of heathenism we shall not dignify as an almost innocent symbolization of the truth! Neither can we wonder at the variety and confusion of these emblematic representations, when we consider that each province and each age would naturally and inevitably embody its own peculiar notions; hence emblems which were worshipped in one district as gods, were held in abhorrence in another. The Greeks and Romans engrafted many of their respective heresies upon the old Egyptian stock. "Gods" unceremoniously borrowed each other's functions and personal deformities, until no marvel that our most enthusiastic and imaginative scholars are bewildered when they attempt to unravel and reconcile the accumulated priestcraft of four thousand years!

So then, we will not attempt to describe the crowd of deities, but will confine our remarks to the character and attributes of Osiris. There is some satisfaction in this investigation, inasmuch as he was the greatest of their gods, and the only one whose worship was universal.

Osiris and Seth (or Typhon) were fabled to be brothers—the children of Seb and Netpe—(Saturn and Rhea). Osiris represented the principle of Good, and his brother that of Evil, and ultimately, that of sin. Now follows the most interesting feature of Egyptian mythology: Osiris is represented to have been put to death by the malice of his brother; but he rose again and became the judge of the dead, and it is in this character that his worship was universally popular in Egypt. The following supposition is hazarded by Sir G. Wilkinson:—"It is evident that Moses abstained from making any pointed allusion to the future state of man, because it would have recalled the well-known Judge of the dead, and all the funereal ceremonies of Egypt," &c. The following scene occurs in a small temple adjoining that of Medinet-Haboo (the Dayr-El-Medinah). Osiris, seated on his throne, awaits the arrival of souls; sundry attendant deities are around; Thoth, the god of Scribes, bears a tablet on which the actions of the dead are recorded, while the other deities are employed in weighing the good deeds against an Ostrich feather; then comes the deceased, bearing the symbol of truth to indicate the purity of his life, &c. A sort of jury of forty-two figures, seated above in two lines, completes this interesting picture.

NEW EXCAVATIONS AT MEDINET-HABOO, THEBES.

In a previous article upon a portion of this temple (the Pylon Gateway, &c.), written on my first journey, occurs the following:—"The place is dreadfully encumbered with heaps of shapeless ruin, and still more with perfect mountains of the debris of deserted Arab towns, under which the farther portions of the great temple are absolutely buried. One can only guess how much more of magnificence and interest might reward the efforts of a vigorous excavating party."

On my late visit, I found that such efforts had been rewarded to the extent which I have now the pleasure to represent. The whole of this fine court, or hall of columns, with a number of lateral ante-chambers, had been excavated by order of the Pasha, whose object in these works was two-fold; first, to stock a fine museum which he has lately erected at Cairo, somewhat after the style of the Crystal Palace, and executed in France; and secondly, to earn the commendations of travellers and of the civilised world. In the first of these objects he has had tolerable success, although, it is to be feared, that a great proportion of the portable valuables discovered find their way into other collections than that at Cairo. I take considerable exception also to the manner in which his works have been executed. In some instances, noble masses of picturesque ruin have been blown to pieces, and removed without any idea of uncovering objects of interest, but simply to clear the space. The material to be removed is, however, chiefly the unburnt brick of Arab ruins, and an incredible accumulation of fine dust. The "hands" employed are generally children, who are "pressed" from the adjoining villages. They carry out the dust in baskets upon their heads, and their movements are continually accelerated by "taskmasters" armed with corbashes, or whips of hippopotamus hide, which are capable of inflicting a terrible stroke. Any one who has attempted to explore a temple whilst it was undergoing this process, will never see any dust worth mentioning elsewhere. At a distance of 50 yards you hear a terrible hubbub, seeing nothing but an impenetrable haze of dust, from which presently emerges, visible at 10 yards, a dust-imp—and another, and a third, and a hundred. Some are staid enough, but for the most part they are merry, impudent little rogues, of an indescribably earthy aspect. One can readily believe these to be descended from a creation originally "of the dust;" but it is difficult to understand how eyes can see, and lungs can breathe, and tongues can clatter in such an element!

Referring to the photograph, the first newly excavated hall which one enters from the doorway in the centre of the picture, contains the bases of 24 noble columns, the centre ones being five or six feet in diameter. The interior walls are covered with finely executed sculptures, chiefly representing the king's offerings to various deities, with the customary interchange of compliments. To this hall succeeds a smaller one, with half the number of columns; and this area is further narrowed in the third court by the width of a chamber on each side. It appears to have only two rows of columns, and no doubt led into the Adytum, which was not yet uncovered at the time of my visit. On the right hand corner of the picture, in the distance, are seen masses of the crude-brick modern ruins, in which the temple has been literally buried. In the centre are two of the great propyla—the upper portions of which have been thrown down—and beneath them is a fine example of a roof of long flat stones. This covers the colonnade of one side of the great court which was represented in a previous picture; and as a few heavy showers of rain fall in most years at Thebes, the joints between the stones were, in some cases, protected by a piece let in along the line of junction, the water being discharged from the outer walls through the projecting mouths of lions. At intervals in these roofs are square apertures, some larger and some smaller. The former probably served as windows, and it has been suggested that the latter were for the purpose of suspending lamps.

NEW EXCAVATIONS AT MEDINET-HABOO, THEBES.

We have previously described some of the scenes which are sculptured upon the interior walls of this beautiful temple; but those on the exterior are no less interesting or important. They are historical subjects, representing the campaigns of the second Rameses, chiefly against his Asiatic enemies. The pictures are divided into compartments, illustrating the progress of affairs. For instance, on the north-east extremity of the wall, trumpeters assemble the troops, who salute the king as he rides past in his chariot. In the next scene he proceeds at a slow pace, attended by fan-bearers, a lion running at the side of the horses. Next compartment, the troops form for the attack; next, the enemy, called "Rebo," await the Egyptians; the king presses forward, bending his bow; several regiments of archers also close in from different points, harassing the enemy with showers of arrows; then ensues a hand-to-hand conflict, and at length the Rebo fly before their victorious aggressors. Heads, tongues, and hands, are brought as returns of the slain. The number, three thousand five hundred and thirty-five, appears as part of the count of hands; but there are two other and larger heaps of hands, and a third of tongues? The king then alights from his chariot, and distributes rewards to his soldiers; and finally, military secretaries draw up accounts of the number of spears, swords, and bows, taken from the enemy. The above is but a specimen of the many elaborate and historically interesting scenes which are found upon the outer walls of the great temple of Medinet-Haboo, of which we have now given our final illustration.

ENTRANCE TO THE GREAT TEMPLE, LUXOR.

WE ought to be very thankful to the man who furnishes a plan of such a place as Luxor. I greatly admire the acumen and the minute acquaintance with the formation and necessities of an Egyptian temple, which are essential for such a work. To restore the original plan of Luxor appears to me to be a piece of comparative anatomical skill equivalent to any of the feats of Cuvier. We have before us a skull very much injured, and a few scraps of the gigantic shank-bones and vertebræ, and these are so much disjointed and scattered that you would never imagine them to be parts of the same mysterious whole: yet Sir Gardner Wilkinson asserts them to be so. Here is his description:—"Luxor, or Lukson, which occupies part of the site of ancient Diospolis, still holds the rank of a market-town. Its name signifies 'the Palaces,' from the temple there erected by Amunoph III. and Rameses II. The former monarch built the original sanctuary and the adjoining chambers, with the addition of the large colonnade and the pylon before it, to which Rameses II. afterwards added the great court, the pyramidal towers, and the obelisks and statues. These, though last in order of antiquity, necessarily form the present commencement of the temple, which, like many others belonging to different epochs, is not two separate edifices, but one and the same building.

"On each side of the entrance is a sitting colossal statue of Rameses II., now buried to the shoulders in the earth and sand accumulated around them. Near the north-west extremity of the propylæ another similar colossus rears its head amidst the houses of the village, which also conceal a great portion of the interesting battle scenes on the front of the towers. The area within, whose dimensions are about 190 feet by 170, is surrounded by a peristyle, consisting of two rows of columns, now almost concealed by hovels and the mosques of the village.

"Passing through the pylon of Amunoph, you arrive at the great colonnade, the length of which, to the next court, is about 170 feet. To this succeeds an area of 155 feet by 167, surrounded by a peristyle of twelve columns in length, and the same in breadth, terminating in a covered portico of thirty-two columns, 57 feet by 111. Behind this is a space occupying the whole breadth of the building, divided into chambers of different dimensions, the centre one leading to a hall supported by four columns, immediately before the entrance to the isolated sanctuary. Behind the sanctuary are two other sets of apartments, the larger ones supported by colonnades, and ornamented with rich sculpture, much of which appears to have been gilded."

This description may appear complicated and interminable to the reader, but I can assure him that it is wonderfully concise and intelligible compared with the impression which the traveller receives from an inspection of the ruins.

The temple was dedicated to Amun, who is represented by the sculptures as addressing the king in the following words:—"Thy government shall continue for millions of years, and we present thee with an eternal pure life." It is also stated that Rameses conquered the Chaldæans, and took 9000 prisoners. He is styled "the Divine Protector, the Conqueror of Nubia. He has destroyed in a second ten millions, and has changed the nations to nothing: no other comes like him."

VIEW AT LUXOR.

LUXOR, reader, is at Thebes; and Thebes, I need hardly say, is an ever present idea with the Nile traveller, from the time that his dahibieh floats out into the broad river from the dirty crowded shore of Boulac, the port of Cairo: and as you listlessly watch the lazy tramp of your sailors, as day after day they "track" your boat in the calm hot weather, or fly before the brisk north winds, your fancy has abundant opportunity for speculation on the history of this mysterious city of the past— its

"Temples, palaces, and piles stupendous,
Of which the very ruins are tremendous."

Thebes was the ancient capital of Upper Egypt, and the groups of antiquities here scattered over a large district, on both sides of the river, are of greater variety and interest than at any other single spot in Egypt. We shall have abundant opportunity, in describing succeeding views, to speak of the history and present aspects of its several divisions: in the meantime we give a map of the district, which will be useful throughout for reference.

The great columns represented in my picture, with the expanded lotus-flower capital, will at once be familiar to every Nile traveller; many of whom I have no doubt, with myself, upon landing at Luxor, have found their anxiety for news from home overpowering for a while their antiquarian enthusiasm, and have hurried past the superb columns in hot haste to the temple of Mustapha-Aga, the native English consular agent, for their letters! Mustapha's abode lies in the shadow on the right of the picture, and he sails into his audience-chamber, in long silken gown and turban, makes his salaam, and hands you all his stock of letters— thirty or forty of them—you can take your choice.

The columns, of which there are twelve, in a double row, were probably erected by Amunoph III, about B.C. 1500. They formed a peristyle of the great Temple, and are about eight feet in diameter, and some thirty to forty feet high. The group of figures in the centre of the picture are natives, who were quarrelling energetically at the moment, and quite unconscious of my designs upon them. The picture was taken in about six seconds.

GRANITE OBELISK AND LOTUS COLUMN, KARNAC.

WHEN one is fairly into "the thick" of the monuments of Thebes, as you are when you stand in the midst of the ruins of the Granite Sanctuary, which this "lotus column" once embellished; when you are here, I say, I recommend you to dismiss the principle of wonder altogether, or you will do nothing but wonder. You will forget to inquire what particular Pharaoh raised this or that monument; your judgment will not be sufficiently cool to recognise, in the quaint figures before you, the evidences of the "finest period of Egyptian art;" and as to the plan of the building, it will never occur to you that the pitiable and perfect chaos of splendid ruin around you ever had any plan. Thanks, however, to the practical mind of Sir G. Wilkinson, I am able to quote from him as follows. After describing the court in front of the Hall of Columns, he says:—"The next court contained two obelisks, the one now standing being 92 feet high and 8 square. Passing between two dilapidated propyla, you enter another smaller area, concealed by a vestibule, in front of the granite gateway of the towers that form the façade of the court before the Sanctuary, which is of red granite, divided into apartments, and surrounded by numerous chambers of small dimensions." This Sanctuary Sir G. Wilkinson considers was originally of sandstone, and even dated before the time of Osirtasin I., but that Thothmes III. (about 1500 B.C.) was the monarch who rebuilt it in this splendid material, syenite, or red granite.

I believe that this obelisk is the most beautiful in Egypt. It will be observed that it has only one row of hieroglyphics on each side, and is said to have been erected by a certain queen, Amun-neit-gori (Nitocris?), about 3300 years ago, and about the time of the flight of Moses from Egypt. Its height, as before stated, is 92 feet, of one block of syenite granite, and consequently was brought from Syene, a distance of about 100 miles. In the quarries at Syene still lies, in situ, an obelisk of nearly similar proportions; and here may be observed the manner in which these blocks were cut. In many instances the well-known method seems to have been adopted of inserting a long line of wooden wedges, which, being saturated with water, split off the block by their pressure in swelling; trenches to receive the water may be observed along the line of the wedge-holes. The "Lotus Column" is an exquisite piece of work; the long slender stalk, and graceful flower of the lotus, were favourite architectural ornaments of the ancient Egyptians: the plant is not now found in Lower Egypt, nor even in Nubia, but is confined to the almost unfrequented solitudes of the Upper Nile. The sculpture on the face of the column presents the pleasing, and as respects Egyptian sculpture, the rare spectacle of the king and his consort in kindly attitude towards each other; and on the right of the picture is part of an interesting tablet, representing, I believe, a coronation scene. Around is a perfect chaos of splendid ruin, amongst which I found it extremely difficult to fix my instruments so as to command a view. May he who finds fault with the arrangement of the picture be dragged to the spot, and compelled to find a better point!

PILLARS IN THE GREAT HALL, KARNAC.

THIS picture represents a few of the pillars of the Hall of Columns, at Karnac. I have taken advantage of the dilapidation of a small part of the outer wall at this point; for from the interior of the hall any photographic representation of this wonderful place is simply impossible, owing to the close juxtaposition of its columns. The effect which the builders appear to have had in view in this remarkable crowding together of enormous columns, is the combined impression of vastness and power—almost of awe—which they produce upon the mind when standing amongst them; and nowhere is this effect attained so perfectly as at Karnac.

The Great Hall is 350 feet long, by 150 broad, and within this noble area are still standing *one hundred and thirty-four* of these colossal columns, the largest of which, forming a double row down the centre, are 75 feet high, and 36 feet in circumference. The capitals of these columns form nearly one-third of their entire height, and have even a greater character than their bases. The roof consists of huge blocks of stone, uniting the capitals, each block having a thickness of seven feet! Such are the witnesses of that ancient dominion, before which even Babylon and Nineveh trembled, and whose victorious armies penetrated to the utmost parts of the then known world, from Ethiopia to Scythia.

Every pillar and every wall of this Great Court is richly adorned with inscriptions and paintings, from which we learn that the founder was Mineptah Seti I., the father of Rameses the Great. The form of Seti is everywhere seen amongst the groups. In one of these we see him presenting offerings to the sovereign deity, Amen Ra, and to the Goddess Athor (another form of Isis or Mut). The accompanying inscription declares that, "This is the visit of the King to the Temple of his Father, the life-dispensing Amen Ra." Above the God Chonsu (the son of Amen) we read, "Thus saith Chonsu in the Thebaïca: 'Come to the Temple, that thou mayest behold thy Father, the King of the Gods.'" Amen, to express his approbation of his son, Seti I., promises him—"I grant thee my dominion, my throne, my possessions, and my duration of life. Have thou rule over Egypt and the Red Land [the peninsula of Sinai], and the Nubians also shall be the footstool beneath thy sandals." In another place the God says, "I grant thee to conquer all nations, that the dread of thee may be in the hearts of the Nubians, and that their kings may come to thee as one man."

Elsewhere in the Hall we behold the God Chonsu receiving reverence, and then embarking in the sacred barge, "to dwell in the Memnoneum of his son, Seti I.," on the opposite side of the Nile.

The southern portion of the Hall of Columns was erected by Rameses II., whose name is repeated innumerable times in its inscriptions. But it is important to observe that the inscriptions and paintings of his predecessors are of a far better style than that of the time of the Great King himself. On the outer wall is a series of some of the most interesting hieroglyphics in all Egypt. They relate to the wars of Seti I., and to those of his son, Rameses II. The former are on the north, and the latter on the south wall. The king, Seti I., appears in a chariot. The enemy are cutting down trees, apparently to build ships with. An inscription underneath runs—"The Great and Mighty of the Armenians speak to praise the Lord of Egypt, and to exalt his valour. Thou art like thy Father, the Sun; we live by thy countenance." In the background is "the Fortress of Kanana"—that is, of Canaan. Above is inscribed, "In the year one of King Seti I. was the campaign undertaken by the army of the king against the Schasu, who were defeated, from the Fortress of Pelusium as far as to the land of Canaan." The Schasu, or Amalekites, are probably the same race who overran Egypt for five hundred years, and who first suffered a defeat, in the year 1593 B.C., by Thothmes III. In 1414 B.C. they were entirely overthrown in a second defeat by Seti I. On this occasion they may be said to have been almost annihilated. Other battles with the Canaanites are also represented; and amongst them appears a nation whose features are of a decidedly Jewish type of countenance.

THE BROKEN OBELISK, &c., KARNAC.

HERE is another glimpse of the grandeur and desolation of Karnac, where there are many acres of magnificent ruin such as we have here represented. When examining these shattered masses, with a view to account for their condition, we could not resist the impression that no force short of the convulsions of earthquakes could have produced some of the indications which we observed—such, for instance, as the huge blocks down the entire face of a mighty pylon wall being split in two, the outer halves having fallen. The obelisk, whose apex appears in my view has very probably been thrown down by a similar convulsion of nature.

These noble monuments, which are so grandly characteristic of old Egyptian architecture, adorned most or all of the cities and temples of antiquity. Some of them doubtless lie buried in the débris of these places, whose sites are now marked only by mountains of hopelessly barren rubbish. Many of them, again, have been removed during long successive centuries to adorn foreign capitals. The one now called Cleopatra's Needle, at Alexandria, was brought from the upper country by the Romans; and a lofty Egyptian obelisk, 116 feet high, once stood in the Campus Martius, at Rome, where it served the purpose of indicator to a gigantic sundial of white marble, on which were hewn figures a yard in length.

One solitary but most interesting obelisk is all that now remains to mark the position of the pontifical city of On, or Heliopolis, the home of Joseph's bride—"Asenath, daughter of Potipherah, priest of On." In front of the temples the obelisks usually stood in pairs, as we still find them at Luxor and Karnac. They were surrounded by lofty flagstaffs, from which floated gorgeous streamers and pennons. Professor Brugsch conjectures that an important object in the erection of the obelisks was the means of ascertaining daily the sun's meridian altitude, and twice annually the solstices.

At the entrance to the Great Hall of Columns, at Karnac, stood two very fine obelisks, both of red Syenite granite. One of them is still standing. It was erected by Thothmes I. in honour of Amun Ra. Not far away stood two others, one of which is standing, and is the finest obelisk now in Egypt. Its companion is the prostrate one which I have photographed. The erect one was raised by the Queen Amen-nempt-Hat-Asu, the sister and guardian of Thothmes III. She is uniformly represented as wearing male attire, and a warrior's helmet. The inscription on the west side of the obelisk is "The Queen of the Diadem, and Benefactor of the year, &c., &c., has erected this as her monument to her father Amun. She has raised to him two beautiful obelisks, and she has decorated them unsparingly and richly with pure gold. She has enlightened Egypt like the Solar Disc. Never has any ruler been comparable to her, the Son (not the daughter) of the Sun, &c." Her name also appears upon the fallen obelisk; but here in many places her surviving brother, Thothmes, has erased her name and inserted his own; and he has even, in one place, claimed for himself the honour of having erected the two obelisks, and of having overlaid them with pure gold.

THE HALL OF COLUMNS, KARNAC.

It is easier, methinks, to write an article for the most insignificant of my subjects than for Karnac: it is perfectly hopeless to attempt to do it justice either by the camera or the pen. I can tell you, it is true, how many columns are standing in the Great Hall, and I can give you their dimensions; but as for transporting you even in imagination to the very spot—as for making you feel the witchcraft of the place, its oppressive grandeur, its dark mysterious interest, the thing is totally impossible. I am even ashamed of any view, it is so thoroughly inadequate to the subject: but the fact is, that the pillars are so strangely crowded together, and their height is so great, as to render it quite impossible to obtain a photograph within the hall itself. The same remark applies to the porticoes of all the Egyptian temples, which are, upon the whole, their most beautiful and striking features. In justice to these glorious ruins, I am bound to confess that these, as well as most of the interiors, I have not been able to illustrate.

From our present point of view, only about two-thirds of the height of the columns is seen, in consequence of an immense accumulation of debris which intervenes. On approaching the hall from this side, the feeling is one of disappointment; it resembles the Pyramids in this respect—that it is not until one descends to their very bases—not until one stands actually amongst them—that their unparalleled magnificence fills the mind.

In connection with other views, I shall speak of the general plans of the principal buildings at Karnac. I now confine myself to a description of the Great Hall, or, as it is commonly called, the Hall of Columns. It measures 329 feet by 170; across the centre stands a double row of pillars, six on each side; their height is 66 feet, without the pedestal and abacus, and they are 12 feet in diameter. I suppose that the total height of the superstructures which they support is not less than 100 feet. On each side of these, ranged in lines, and standing, I think, not more than 6 or 8 feet apart, are 122 others, each 41 feet 9 inches high, and 27 feet 6 inches in circumference. There is no roof, but the pillars are connected by single blocks of stone, of prodigious dimensions. The two great pillars shown in my Photograph, standing at the eastern extremity of the hall, were partly built into the outer wall, as appears from the stones on this side having been left rough for that purpose. Sir G. Wilkinson says that the lintel stones of the portal which stood between these were 40 feet 9 inches in length. This hall was commenced by Osirei, and finished by his son Rameses the Great, about 1400 years before Christ. All the pillars and the walls, both externally and internally, are completely covered with sculpture—some of it in bas-relief—in the most finished style of this the finest period of Egyptian art, and it was all originally brilliantly coloured; not much, however, of this colouring now remains.

SCULPTURED GATEWAY, KARNAC.

Hast thou already forgotten, O reader, that we have given on a previous page a sketch map of Thebes? I recommend frequent reference to this map, because I recollect that, as I approached that celebrated capital of yore, on the tiptoe of expectation, my mental gyrations with regard to its geography were painfully ludicrous. Karnac, Luxor, the Memnonium, Medinet-Haboo, Goornah—each and all first appeared to me to be on one side of the river, then on the other. Thebes, the city, was on the site of Karnac, and presently it was miles away at Medinet-Haboo; until at length, absorbed in contemplation of the temple ruins, I well-nigh forgot that a mighty city, quite independent of these suburban embellishments, had existed at all. Let us stand, therefore, upon the principal site of the ancient city, of which scarcely a vestige remains. We are on the western bank of the river (the right-hand side when ascending), looking north towards Cairo. A rich alluvial plain, of some twenty square miles in extent, bounded on each side by limestone hills, and intersected by the river, spreads all around. Immediately in front of us is the old temple of Goornah, scarcely peeping out of the tamarisk groves which surround it, and indeed being the least pleasing of the ruins of Thebes. Bearing round to the left, until the eye reaches the mountains, we see opposite Goornah the entrance to the Valley of the Tombs of the Kings. Further to the left, on the slope of the barren hills—here covered with innumerable caves and mounds, the evidences of ancient sculpture—stand the ruins of the temple called the Memnonium, or Rameseum. Behind us, still following the western hills, is the temple palace of Medinet-Haboo, covering a wonderful space of ground, but almost buried in the mud ruins of a deserted Arab town. Then in the plain, still behind, but nearer to us, stand the two prodigious statues of Memnon. Now, passing over the river, close to its banks on the south, we see the Temple of Luxor, and the considerable modern village, with its mosque, which has grown up about it; and lastly, wheeling round to our original position, we see at a great distance in the north, towards our right hand, towering over extensive groves of dark green palms, the ruins of Karnac.

Returning to our boat at Luxor, I consider that we are in a position to land and start fair for Karnac. And whilst our donkeys are nimbly plying their patient, "many twinkling feet" over the cultivated land, for the first mile of our journey, I will tell you that Karnac was originally the site of one or two modest, square-pillared temples, built, perhaps, about the time of Osirtasin I., some 1800 years before our era, and a little before the arrival of Joseph in Egypt. To these, succeeding monarchs, each endeavouring to surpass his predecessors in the magnitude and splendour of his monuments, built and added, until the entire group of sacred buildings embraced five or six distinct temples, which were finally surrounded by a vast crude brick wall, enclosing about two square miles of ground. In this wall were placed, by the Ptolemies, or Greek kings of Egypt (B.C. 300 to B.C. 14), four magnificent gateways, of the most beautiful of which—the one which we are now approaching from Luxor—I stop to give a Photograph. But I should premise that we have advanced for 200 or 300 yards through a dromos, or avenue of recumbent sphynxes, now all mutilated and headless. The block on the left of the gateway in the picture represents one of them. They had the heads of rams and a figure of the king before the fore feet. Such an avenue once led to each of the principal gateways of the sacred enclosures, one of them being continued as far as Luxor, about a mile and a half. I judge this beautiful pylon, or gateway, to be about 60 feet high; it was erected by Ptolemy Euergetes, A.D. 246. Dr. Brutsch gives the following translation of its principal inscription:—"The king, the son of the beneficent of gods, who has been chosen by the sun, and is the living portrait of Amun, the son of the sun, the lord of diadems, the immortal Ptolemais, the beloved of the god Ptah, has erected this door as his monument for his sublime father, Amun Ra, the lord of the throne of worlds, the first in Thebes—the great god, the lord of heaven, of earth, of water, and of mountains. He has made the wings of this door from sandal-wood, the bars of pure gold, and all the nails of iron. Euergetes the First has dedicated this door not only to Amun Ra, but also to the god Chonsu, the son of Amun, and the goddess Maut."

VIEW AT KARNAC, FROM THE GRANITE PYLON.

THE extensive and massive ruins of Karnac are the remains of temples and palaces erected throughout such a long succession of ages, and by so many dynasties of Egyptian and foreign monarchs, that the associations which throng around them are not merely those of Egypt alone, but also of the whole ancient world. In many cases individual courts and columns in its temples contain inscriptions and decorations wrought at the command of sovereigns separated from one another by the interval of more than a thousand years. Some of these still remain almost as entire as when they received their finishing touches; others are wholly dilapidated, and reduced to shapeless mounds of rubbish; sufficient, however, remains to afford long occupation to the most indefatigable explorers. Champollion, Lepsius, and Brugsch, all made these temples their abode for weeks or months. The latter thus describes his arrival at Karnac:—"On the evening of my arrival I took up my abode in the Temple of Ape or Apet. When I had retired to rest, I was favoured with a nocturnal concert: a number of jackals had quitted their lurking-places, and were beginning their dismal howlings in the surrounding courts and colonnades; overhead I was disturbed by the whirring and ghost-like flight of a whole flock of squeaking bats, which, during the day-time, had concealed themselves in the crevices of my chamber." This Temple of Apc (the next in importance to the great temple of Amun Ra) was erected by "King Ptolemy Energetes II., his sister Cleopatra, and his wife Cleopatra, to the goddess Ape, the Great Mother of the gods, the Queen of heaven, the Ruler of the earth, the Honoured in the Province of Thebes." On the southern side of the same temple is a wall raised by the Roman Emperor Augustus. He is styled "The Sun and Lord of both worlds, the Autocrat, the Son of the sun and Lord of the Diadem, Cæsar, who renders the Provinces happy under his authority."

But the chief portion of Karnac is occupied by the Great Temple of Amun, a very interesting portion of which is called the Temple of Ramases III. Amongst the inscriptions contained in it is the following:—"In the year VI., in the month Paoni, his Majesty commanded that the gifts to his father, Amun Ra, King of the gods, on his altar of offerings, should be increased with much gold and incense. Thus commanded King Ramases III." Still more worthy of notice are the interiors of the most sacred shrines in the Great Temple. These shrines are built of granite, and contain representations of "Pilipus, the King and Son of the sun," i.e. Philip Aridæus. They are only partially finished. Near these shrines are inscriptions by the Ethiopian kings Sebabak and Taharah from the "Land of the Negroes," i.e. Ethiopia. Others mention the tribute brought by Shishak (Sebeshenk) from the Land of Syria into Egypt. On the north wall of this temple is a series of inscriptions which contains repeated mention of the Assyrians, Babylonians, Mesopotamians, Syrians, and Ethiopians; also of parts of Palestine. In one of these inscriptions it is recorded:—"In the year XI. was brought the tribute of the King of As-su-ri (Assur), a great stone of lapis-lazuli, weighing twenty minæ and nine asses, beautiful lapis-lazuli from Bade-li (Tabel), and the coverings of vases from As-su-ri, &c."

In one of the groups on the walls of the Temple of Amun the traveller is reminded of the "Ark of the Covenant" mentioned in the Pentateuch, and of the priests who bore it in sacred procession, for a similar ark is here represented, also carried by a number of the priests.

Amongst the conquests of Amenotoph II. is mentioned one gained over the people of Nineveh. And amongst the inscriptions probably belonging to the reign of the same monarch is the interesting representation of an embassy from the Phoenicians, who are delineated as having ruddy complexions, and with bearded faces. Their leader appears as spokesman, and those behind him are bearing presents or tribute. Their address is—"We the ancient and noble of the Phoenicians thus speak: 'Incline thine ear, O King of the Egyptians, and Son of the Nubians! May great reverence be rendered to thee! We knew nothing of Egypt, neither had our forefathers entered it, but we have become sensible of thy beneficence, and may all nations be as thy footstool!'"

COURT OF SHISHAK, THEBES.

PROFESSOR BRUTSCH furnishes the following interesting information in illustration of this picture:—"The court of Shishak (also called the Hall of the Bubastic Kings) is one of the apartments of the magnificent range of halls and colonnades forming the Temple of Amon at Karnac. It abounds in inscriptions of a peculiarly interesting character, and was dedicated to Amon-Ra by the king, Sheshonk I., the Shishak of Holy Scripture. We constantly meet with representations of Shishak and his deceased favourite son, the Prince Sha-pant, 'the First Prophet of Amon-Ra-Sontor, the commander of the infantry and prefect of the South.' The monarchs of Egypt, from the twenty-first dynasty onwards, united in themselves the title of king with that of "First Prophet of Amon-Ra, the King of the Gods." All the inscriptions in the Hall of Shishak relate to the reign of himself and his own posterity. On the exterior wall of this court is the celebrated list of the various monarchs and nations who submitted to Shishak during his expedition against Palestine. We read (2 Chron. xii. 2-4, 9), 'And it came to pass that in the fifth year of King Rehoboam, Shishak king of Egypt came up against Jerusalem, because they had transgressed against the Lord, with twelve hundred chariots and three score thousand horsemen; and the people were without number that came with him out of Egypt; the Lubims, the Sukkiims, and the Ethiopians. And he took the fenced cities which pertained to Judah, and came to Jerusalem.' 'So Shishak, king of Egypt, came up against Jerusalem, and took away the treasures of the house of the Lord, and the treasures of the king's house; he took all; he carried away also the shields of gold which Solomon had made.'

"The record of Scripture is confirmed by the inscriptions at Karnac; for in the court of Shishak we find the names of one hundred and thirty-three conquered cities and nations, and amongst them is recorded the name 'Joudah Melek Kah' (the king of the country of Judah). There are also the names of many of the 'fenced' and other cities of Palestine, and amongst them those of Re-bi-ta, or Rabbith; Ta-en-kau, or Taanach; Schen-ma-oa, or Shemen; Bit-schen-raa, or Bethshan; Ha-qe-re-ma, or Haphraim; Beit-duaren, or Beth-horon; Kattem, or Kedem; and Maketau, or Megiddo. Accompanying the inscription of 'King of the country of Judah' is a portrait of the same monarch, bearing the unmistakable physiognomy of a Hebrew, and with his hands represented as bound behind him, to indicate his entire conquest and submission. As in the case of the great Rameses II., so also we find Sesostris represented as of gigantic stature and seizing his enemies collectively, so as to dispatch them at one blow. 'The goddess of the Thebaid, the Queen of Power, the ruler of all nations,' stands by him, figurative of the vast power and extended dominion of Shishak, by which the fear of him spread through all the nations of the then known world. The god Amon addresses him, 'My heart is filled with exceeding joy whilst I behold thy victories, thou my beloved son Amon-mer-Sheshonk; I have begotten thee for my own honour.' The inscription continues at great length, and in it the god further praises the king because he has erected temples to his honour at Thebes, Hermonthis, and Heliopolis."

The single column still standing is the sole remaining representative of an avenue of twelve which once adorned this court. Sir G. Wilkinson suggests that from the breadth of the intercolumniation, and the proportionate smallness of the columns, they were not intended to support a roof, nor even architraves, but rather to bear hawks or other similar emblems. The opinion of our party, from a careful examination of the fractures of the stones, &c., in this part of the ruins, was that these dilapidations, and the chevaux-like disposal of the fragments of the columns in the foreground of the picture, are the result of the shock of an earthquake.

VIEW IN THE INTERIOR OF THE HALL OF COLUMNS, KARNAC.

BEFORE I ascended the Nile, a photographic friend, whom I met at Cairo, discouraged me greatly about Karnac. The place, he said, was impregnable—that it was idle to plant a camera against it—such vast and shapeless masses of ruin packed together as tight as it would stow, and built in on all sides with tremendous blank walls. I say I was discouraged; nevertheless, I brought up my artillery boldly, and fired away right and left—with what success I leave my readers to judge—and yet I think my friend's representations must have somewhat unmanned me; for on my first journey I attempted no interior view of the great hall, which is the chief ornament and wonder of Karnac, and indeed of Egypt. On the contrary, I wrote that "the pillars are so strangely crowded together, and their height is so great, as to render it quite impossible to obtain a photograph within the hall itself!" But if the reader will turn back (six pictures) he will find that I crept round the outer wall, and took advantage of dilapidations therein effected by some former warrior, obtaining a shot across the hall, which was not altogether ineffective. And whilst the reader is there, he may perhaps like to revise what is said about this great hall. Think of the dimensions—350 feet long, by 150. One hundred and thirty-four columns, such as are here represented, still standing. The centre avenue 75 feet high, and 36 feet in circumference. Why, there is many a snug little sitting-room not more than 12 feet square: the base of one of those columns would not stand in its area!

Well, on my late journey I seem to have recovered my self-possession. But I will relate how, step-by-step, I forced the enemy's positions. First, as my cavalcade of donkeys and Arabs (designedly so placed gentle reader!) pattered along from Luxor in a whirlwind of dust, I sounded a hasty "halt!" as we neared the beautiful pylon gateway of the Ptolemaic period, and although by no means regardless of the grim old sphynxes that guard it, I planted my engines, and "took the approaches." Then I entered the sacred enclosure, turned sharp round to the right, and carried off the pair of huge fellows who flank the remains of the glorious "Granite Pylon." Wheeling round my tackle, I possessed myself of an extent of the most deplorably ruinous territory that the world knows (see Supplementary Volume, 21st View), and then I approached the enemy's stronghold—that great centre of temples and shrines, whose nucleus was formed nearly 4000 years ago, and to which a period of twenty centuries added its industry and its wealth. Passing under the great unfinished pylon, I entered the "Court of Shishak," and welcomed into the fore-ground of my picture those cheese-like piles of prostrate column-stones, which have been the delight of artists from time immemorial, but which the enlightened governor of Egypt has lately entirely swept away, that he might have a clear carriage-drive through the temple! Then, burning with ambition—yet with much fearfulness—I entered that dark vista which you see in the centre of my last picture, and turning down one of the side aisles, I pointed my camera at a double line of those dingy old immensities—indestructible—indescribable, and hitherto deemed impossible! Not so! I trust the reader will consider that I obtained a worthy picture to close our volume upon Egypt, and that he will do me the pleasure to accompany me through my further travels in Nubia and Ethiopia.—Farewell!

www.ingramcontent.com/pod-product-compliance
Lightning Source LLC
Chambersburg PA
CBHW020259090426
42735CB00009B/1144